POISONED

ISBN: 978-1-941914-20-5
Typesetting and Design by Christopher Boynton
Saltimbanque Books, New York
www.saltimbanquebooks.com
www.jboyett.net

POISONED

J. BOYETT

Saltimbanque Books

New York

For Leo.

BY THE SAME AUTHOR

Amy Madden

Brothel

Daughter of the Damned

Ironheart

The Little Mermaid: A Horror Story

The Man Who Fed Myagg'daggeth

Raw Flesh, Cold Air

Ray Takeshi and the Medallions of Skarth

Resilient Creatures

Ricky

The Sexbot

Stewart and Jean

The Switch

Tusk

The Unkillables

The Victim and Other Short Plays

ACKNOWLEDGMENTS

I'd like to thank all those listed in the Production Histories, as well as Brandi Varnell, Kathryn McConnell's partner in Squeaky Bicycle.

POISONED

Historical Note

Nothing brings home to me the passage of time since this play premiered, as the way language has since changed. Back in 2011, Dee-Dee's use of the word "vibe" did feel anachronistic. Now, in 2025, it's back in general circulation. For example, in the phrase "vibe shift," which gets bandied about to describe our current political turmoil.

Production History

Poisoned was commissioned by Squeaky Bicycle Productions for their Winter Reading Lab and had its first developmental reading on February 27, 2011.

SAM: Kelly Kay Griffith
TOM: William Kozy
DEE-DEE: Mandy Nicole Moore
STAGE DIRECTIONS: Kerry Kastin
Directed by Kathryn McConnell.

Poisoned had its premiere production as an AEA Showcase at the Mint Theatre space, from November 19 to December 10, 2011.

SAM: Kelly Kay Griffith
TOM: Dennis Brito
DEE-DEE: Kate Eastman
Directed by Kathryn McConnell.

Poisoned had its second production during the 2013 Midtown Theatre Festival, from July 18 to July 28, 2013.

SAM: Mary Sheridan
TOM: Mark Armstrong
DEE-DEE: Hannah Jane McMurray
Directed by Michael Hagins.

Characters:

SAM, 40's.
TOM, 40's.
DEE-DEE, 20's.

Setting:

TOM's living room, somewhere in Colorado.

POISONED

Lights up on Tom's living room. The front door opens and Tom and Sam enter, with Sam's suitcases. Sam looks around the living room.

SAM

This is a nice house, Tom.

TOM

Thank you.

SAM

My big brother finally made good.

TOM

At long last, I've won my little sister's approval.

SAM

So. You like it here in Colorado?

TOM

I moved out here, didn't I?

SAM

For work, though. You didn't just up and move here. You were sent.

TOM

Sure, but I wouldn't have let them transfer me if I hadn't liked the place. Besides, what's not to like?

SAM

It's very pretty.

TOM

You haven't seen anything yet. Just the drive here from the airport, that's nothing. Tonight we'll take you out to dinner, then tomorrow we'll go out driving and show you the mountains. Just the three of us, you, me, and Dee-Dee.

SAM

Riiight ... you, me, and Dee-Dee.... Why wasn't Dee-Dee with you at the airport, again?

TOM

I told you, she had to register for classes.

SAM

Oh, that's right.

TOM

It's not like she didn't want to be there to meet you. It's just, today was registration day.

SAM

I totally understand.

TOM

So. You like Manhattan?

SAM

It's not a matter of liking it. That's where I work, is all.

TOM

Yeah, but do you like it?

SAM

I like working. Yeah, I like it there. Sure.

TOM

It sure is different from where we grew up.

SAM

So's here.

TOM

I guess so.... Dee-Dee's really interested in your work.

SAM

Is she.

TOM

Sure. I mean, she wants to be a writer. And she's talented. I think so, anyway. But she doesn't know much about, you know, the technical, professional side of all that. So I think it's a good opportunity for her, getting to sit down with an entertainment lawyer and pick her brain.

SAM

Mm. At this stage maybe it would behoove her more to worry about learning her craft, than it would to learn the ins and outs of intellectual property law.

TOM

Well, of course. Naturally. I mean, Dee-Dee hasn't been talking about wanting to pick your brain. That's just an idea that occurred to me. I haven't even mentioned it to her.

SAM

Okay.

TOM

What, are you getting uptight about this?

SAM

I didn't fly out to Colorado to have my brain picked by Dee-Dee.

TOM

I know you didn't.

SAM

If possible I would prefer to have no parts of my body picked at all.

TOM

All right! I guess I picked—I mean, excuse me, *chose* an unfortunate phrase. I guess what I meant by "have your brain picked" was "at some point have a casual conversation about your area of expertise." But we can make even *that* off-limits, if you prefer. Jesus!

SAM

Why are you yelling at me?

TOM

I'm not *yelling*, I'm....

SAM

You're raising your voice.

(Pause.)

TOM

Yes. I am raising my voice. I didn't mean to. I'm sorry.

SAM

It's all right.

TOM

Hey, listen, Samantha. When was the last time we got together and didn't fight?

SAM

We're not fighting.

TOM

Just about.

SAM

We're not.

TOM

We are.

SAM

No we're not.

TOM

Jesus!... I guess what I'm trying to say is, I was excited when you called to say you were coming. I was moved, even. Because we, I mean, we're not *old*, or anything. But we are, you know, uh ... not kids. I mean, life goes fast. I love you. And I've always assumed that one day some big thing would happen between us that would fix all our problems. There's always been this tension, but I've always had this belief that one day some big dramatic event would take place, and it would all go away. Be cured. But lately, I've been getting ... life goes by so fast. It is so, so fast. This amazing healing thing that's going to happen between me and Sam: when is it going to get here? It better hurry.... I've been thinking that for quite a while now, dwelling on it these last months. So when you called to say you were coming out all of a sudden, that you'd found a cheap last-minute flight and were coming out to spend time with me and Dee-Dee, it felt like a sign. Like maybe this was it.... It moved me, Sam.

SAM

I came to see you, Tom. Not Dee-Dee, so much.

TOM

Yeah, well. She's *with* me, Sam.

SAM

I don't mean that I expect her to keep out of sight, I just mean that naturally my brother is the main person I'm here to see.

TOM

Right. I guess I thought getting to know Dee-Dee might be part of your motivation for coming out. Since I am in love with her, and all.

SAM

Mm, yes, you mentioned that.

TOM

Yes. I'm sure I probably did. Anyway. If you don't want to turn into bosom buddies right this weekend, hey, that's cool. Please do keep in mind that this is her house, too, though—

SAM

Well, she *lives* here, because you *let* her—

TOM

This is her house too, and there's not going to be any cold-shoulder bullshit. Got it?

SAM

You don't have to give me any lectures on etiquette, big brother.

TOM

Oh, don't worry, I know that's another of your areas of expertise....

SAM

"I am deeply in love with Dee-Dee." You know, I do worry about you, Tom. Because with most men, these sorts of fevers wind down soon enough. You're in love, you're in love, and then all of a sudden you get a chance to fuck someone even younger, or just someone different. And then this person you've been making all these declarations of love to is nothing but an extremely inconvenient obstacle. You have to get rid of her, without of course being a bad guy yourself. You have to somehow persuade her to be reasonable, and understand that all those big words, while they weren't exactly lies, they weren't necessarily meant to be taken literally, either. She's suddenly this excitable bag of nerves who takes everything to heart, and your friends commiserate with you over how hard it must be to let a person like that down easy, when she doesn't want to cooperate.... Am I right? Is that not the way it is, with men?

TOM

That's usually the way it is, yeah.

SAM

And it's been that way with you before.

TOM

It has. I didn't say I was the nicest guy.

SAM

What I'm saying is that you're still not.

TOM

And what I'm saying is that that's how I know things are different with Dee-Dee. Is because none of that has happened.

SAM

Not yet. Maybe your reactions are just getting slower, in your old age.

TOM

Me and Dee-Dee are getting married, Sam.

SAM

Well. Maybe that'll be the thing, that does the trick. Maybe you'll say "I do," and then look at her, and realize that that feverish love feeling is gone, that it's dead and you're free of it. That would be a kind of a happy ending.

TOM

Gee, why don't we hang out more often?

SAM

Because we always hurt each other.

TOM

You've had a lot of disappointments. But I get tired of you taking them out on me.

SAM

What if I really am trying to help you?

TOM

It works out to the same thing. You hurt me, Sam. You're hurting me.

SAM

I'm sorry.... But really, Tom. What do you know about this girl?

TOM

What is it I'm supposed to know?

SAM

Her history. Her past.

TOM

As you were just pointing out, she's too young to have much of either.

SAM

It doesn't take much time. A lot can happen in a year. Or a month. Or a week. Or a weekend. It might only take twenty minutes for someone to do the kind of thing her future husband would be very interested in knowing about. What do you know about her? She's from Plano, Texas. She went to college for, like, a week, in Dallas. The rest is just a vague list of places she spent time wandering around in—a few months in Tulsa, some time in Miami, a trip to California.

TOM

I can't believe you remember all this stuff. Why do you remember all this?

SAM

You told it to me.

TOM

Yeah, but why do you remember it?

SAM

I remember things that I think pertain to my brother's future happiness.

TOM

Well, what the hell are you trying to say she was doing during those unfilled-in years? Being a spy? You have some paranoid fantasy that's run away with you....

SAM

So I'm paranoid, huh. So you think it's so impossible that your little angel might ever have done something that you'd prefer not to know about.

TOM

No, that's the whole point—I would prefer not to know about it. I'm sure she's done crazy, dumb stuff. She's probably even done some distasteful stuff. God knows I've done things that I'd be mortified if Dee-Dee found out about them. Or if you did. So, thank God you won't find out. People have a right to their secrets.

SAM

Maybe you're just scared of what you might find out.

TOM

Yeah. Uh-huh. Okay, fine. You know what, Sam? You're scared of being useless. You think if there's not some practical reason for me to have you around, I won't want you. So you make up all this shit about how you're on a big mission to save me from myself, as an excuse to come and visit. But the truth is that you could just come visit. You don't need a reason. *I* don't need a reason to want to see you. In fact, we'd all be better off without the reasons you come up with.

SAM

This isn't about me, sorry. This is about you, throwing your life away.

TOM

Samantha, I'm telling you that I'm in love and that I'm going to get married. You don't have to be so mournful about it.

SAM

Oh, I suppose I should be jumping up and down for joy, right?

TOM

Uh, yeah! That would actually be the traditional reaction! Some sisters, if their brothers told them "Hey, after years of searching I've found happiness," some sisters would be like, "That's good! That's really nice!"

SAM

Yeah, well, some sisters have to worry less about their brothers than I do, I guess.

TOM

Oh, Jesus. It's not your job to worry about me! Your job is to let me live my own life. If you also would like to share in my joys, and in my sorrows, that would be great. That would be what I prefer. But if you can't do that, if the very best you can do is to leave me alone, and quietly disapprove, from a distance.... Well. That's up to you.

SAM

So I'm supposed to "share" in this "joy." I'm supposed to be thrilled that my brother and some, some kid, that he knows nothing about....

TOM

Hey. You're going to have to watch what you say about Dee-Dee, in front of me.

SAM

You want to know the real reason I flew out here? Was to warn you about Dee-Dee.

(Pause.)

TOM

Was to warn me about Dee-Dee. And here I thought you just missed me.

SAM

I care about you. I look after you.

TOM

You look after me.

SAM

I sure do. And I gotta say, it feels like a pretty thankless job sometimes.

TOM

I should thank you.

SAM

Someday, you will.

TOM

You know what I wish I could thank you for? Just flying out here to share my life with me, as an equal. Instead of rushing around like a busy little bee, babysitting me.

SAM

Yeah, well. Anyway. It looks like I got here in the nick of time. I hope you were at least going to sign a pre-nup?

TOM

Jesus, Samantha....

SAM

She dropped out of school, she spent a few years gallivanting around God knows where doing God knows what, and now she's flitted her way here and has decided to live off you while she goes back to school, on a whim. That's all you know about this kid.

TOM

She doesn't live *off* me, she lives *with* me.

SAM

Oh, and I suppose you guys split the house payment and all the expenses.

TOM

No, I pay for most of them, because I earn a lot more money than she can. But there's nothing sinister about it. She hasn't tricked me or anything.

SAM

She's just a kid, Tom. Do you really believe you can trust her?

TOM

Okay, I know this isn't very politically correct, but: there's a lot to be said for youth. Forty may be the new twenty, but frankly the new twenty has got nothing on the old twenty. It's like New Coke. I like young people. I like people who are younger than me and I like having a girlfriend who's younger than me. It's not because I have a neurotic, pathetic need to recapture my own youth. It's because young people—or, at least, young people like Dee-Dee—they still have that energy, that good humor. She's not afraid of things, and I like how her recklessness rubs off on me. She's still fresh. She hasn't been corrupted yet.

SAM

She hasn't been corrupted yet.

TOM

That's right. Not that you and I are so corrupted, but ... well, we are.

SAM

Uh-huh. Big brother, you are so naive.

TOM

Okay, look, I told you to cut that shit out....

SAM

You know why I flew out here? I flew out here to *tell* you something, about Dee-Dee.

TOM

To tell me something?... I hear her car pulling in.

SAM

Oh, by "her" car do you mean the car that you bought for her?

TOM

Say whatever you've got to say quick, before she comes in.

SAM

Oh, no. *This* is going to take a *while*.

TOM

Come on. Quit screwing around.

SAM

And when I tell you what it is, you're going to thank me for it.

(Enter Dee-Dee.)

DEE-DEE

Sam?!

SAM

Dee-Dee, I presume?

DEE-DEE

(running over and hugging Sam)

It's so great to finally meet you!

SAM

Well, it's good to meet you, too.

DEE-DEE

You guys been catching up?

TOM

Oh, sure. It's like we're able to pick right back up where we always leave off.

DEE-DEE

That's great. Did you talk about, um ... stuff?

SAM

We did, actually, yes.

DEE-DEE

You did?!

SAM

I'm sorry, I was being facetious. I guess my sarcastic joke was that everything is "stuff," so naturally we were talking about "stuff."

DEE-DEE

Oh.

SAM

I'm sorry, it wasn't—I didn't mean—I guess I was just trying to make a joke, I wasn't trying to be, you know.

TOM

One thing that Samantha is really good at is pointing out little mistakes like that, honey. Or, sorry, I don't guess we should really call it a "mistake," it's more like just a ... shit, what should we call it, Sam? A vagary? An inexactness of speech?

SAM

What my big brother is trying to say is that I'm a bitch.

(Pause.)

DEE-DEE

So. Did you talk about ... um.... Did you tell her?

TOM

Tell her what?

DEE-DEE

Tom!

TOM

Oh! About us getting married?

DEE-DEE

Yes!

TOM

I'm sorry, honey, I'm a little frazzled is all.

(Pause.)

DEE-DEE

So you *told* her?!

TOM

Yes, yes, yes! I did, I actually just before you came in had just got done telling her.

DEE-DEE

Well ... well, hey, wow, what do you, you know, what do you think?

SAM

It doesn't really matter what *I* think.

DEE-DEE

Of course it does!

SAM

Well. In that case, "congratulations" is what I think.

DEE-DEE

(taking Sam's hands)

Thank you. Sam, I want things to be ... I want.... There's, um, some champagne in the kitchen! Can I get the champagne? Is that okay? I mean, I know it's before dinner, and we still have to drive to the restaurant, but maybe....

TOM

One glass apiece of champagne won't hurt us. Don't you think so, Sam? Don't you agree that champagne is in order?

SAM

Sure.

DEE-DEE

I'll get it!

(Exit Dee-Dee.)

TOM

Okay, let's start over, all right? And no more of that stuff we were talking about before. You can see how she's making an effort.

SAM

But can't you at least entertain the possibility that I might be right? What if there really is something about her that you don't know, that you would like to know?

TOM

I don't want to know it.

SAM

But what if it turns out that you're fooling yourself?

TOM

That's probably the main thing all happy people have in common. Is that they're fooling themselves.

SAM

I want to help you.

TOM

I know you do, Sam. And that's what I'm asking you to do. Is to help me. By not trying to spoil things.

(Pause.)

SAM

Okay.

(Dee-Dee returns with champagne, glasses, she hands them over, pours, etc.)

DEE-DEE

This is exciting!

TOM

Yeah. It is.

SAM

Sure.

DEE-DEE

You know what? I kind of never thought I'd get married.

SAM

Oh really? Why's that?

DEE-DEE

Just not for me. I didn't think I was the type. It's so *traditional,* I always thought it sounded boring.

SAM

But ol' Tom changed your mind.

DEE-DEE

Yeah.

TOM

I turned on the charm.

DEE-DEE

Did you ever get married, Samantha?

SAM

I think Tom or I would have mentioned it by now if I had a husband, Dee-Dee.

DEE-DEE

I thought you might have gotten married and divorced, by now.

SAM

Nope. I wasn't as lucky as you. I never met a man who swept me off my feet, I guess.

TOM

Well, I wouldn't say I swept her off her feet. Much as I wish I could say it. I offered her some stability, is all.

DEE-DEE

That's not all you offered, you dork! Although it is a pretty cool part of things. I spent a lot of time sort of wandering around all over the place.

SAM

Yeah, Tom told me. Apparently you caught quite the travel bug.

DEE-DEE

Well. The whole time I was growing up my biggest ambition was just to leave town, you know? I was always like, "God, get me the fuck *out* of here!" I really wanted to go to college out of state. I fantasized about moving off and going to some big famous school like Notre Dame or Harvard or someplace off in New York somewhere, but, you know, my grades sucked. So I wound up at school in *Dallas.* And I'd grown up just a few miles away in Plano. Like, the campus was practically down the street from where I'd grown up, so I had to keep living with my fucking parents. So I was like, What's the *point?* Finally I realized that I didn't need an out-of-state school as an excuse to move out. I didn't need any excuse at all. So I told my parents I was going to quit school and leave town. They freaked out. So I was like, "Okay! Okay! Never mind!" Then the next day I left the house with all my money without telling them and I got my friend to pick me up and take me to the Greyhound station, and I took off.

SAM

Your parents must have been worried.

DEE-DEE

Yeah. They were pretty pissed. But, you know—I mean, I'd *tried* just talking about it with them, and they'd freaked out. So I figured, "What else am I supposed to do?"

TOM

Dee-Dee here didn't even know where she was going until she was at the ticket window. Can you believe that? I can't imagine having the guts to just throw myself upon the mercy of the universe like that.

SAM

Huh. Yeah.... So where did you wind up going?

DEE-DEE

I bought a ticket to LA. I'd always sort of wanted to be an actress.

SAM

Ah. Okay. So you chose where you were going to go totally at random, but even so, you didn't wind up anyplace *too* unusual.

DEE-DEE

I guess not, no.

SAM

And did you become an actress?

DEE-DEE

Well, not really. I mean, otherwise you would know.

SAM

Not necessarily. There are all kinds of actresses. All different levels. It's not like you go to a couple of auditions and suddenly you're famous.

TOM

She knows that, Sam.

DEE-DEE

Yeah. I didn't mean that you'd know because I'd be famous. I just meant that you would know, because Tom would have told you.

SAM

Ah. Okay. So what did you wind up doing in LA? Or did you just kind of pass through?

DEE-DEE

No, I stayed for a few months. I sort of went to auditions and stuff, but I didn't really know what I was doing. So I just kind of hung out. I wound up living with some guy and stuff.

SAM

Living with some guy. Like, someone you knew from back home? Who also happened to be out in LA?

DEE-DEE

Well, no. Someone I met out there.

TOM

Don't worry, Dee-Dee, Sam knows about co-habitation. Like that guy Peter that you used to live with?

SAM

Right. It turned into a big mess when I found out he was cheating on me, because he refused to be the one to go look for a new apartment, he wanted us to keep living together as roommates.

TOM

Ah. That's right. I guess that was kind of a, um, awkward thing to bring up.

DEE-DEE

That guy sounds like a real dick-cheese.

SAM

A what?

DEE-DEE

A dick-cheese.... You know—dick-cheese?

(Pause. Sam and Tom have never heard the term "dick-cheese.")

SAM

Anyway. Of course, I was twenty-five before I moved in with a guy. Not right out of high school.

DEE-DEE

Does that make a difference?

SAM

No. No. Sorry. Anyway. So LA didn't pan out.

DEE-DEE

And then I've just been moving around from place to place. I've lived all over, now. Which was what I'd always wanted, right? But it gets old. At first it's this big huge crazy-ass adventure! But then after a while it's just the same old exact adventure, over and over again. I've lived in LA, and San Francisco, and New York, and Atlanta, and Miami, and I was in Mexico for a little while which was awesome, but it just felt so dangerous, and I lived in Flagstaff for a while, and Boston. Oh, and Montana.

SAM

That's a lot of places to have lived in by the time you're—how old are you, exactly?

DEE-DEE

Twenty-two.

SAM

Wow.

TOM

Dee-Dee, honey, I think my little sister is worried about the age difference between us. She's afraid I'm a hardened old man of the world taking advantage of you, the sweet innocent babe in arms.

DEE-DEE

Oh—well—don't worry about that....

SAM

No, no, no, I just would have guessed you were older.... Maybe it's because you're so mature.

DEE-DEE

I *have* had a lot of experiences, I guess.

SAM

So, I'm fascinated. You would just randomly move to these places, and then what?

DEE-DEE

Oh, just get a job. Usually some random shit job in a shop somewhere.

SAM

And would you often move in with a guy right away? Like you did in LA?

DEE-DEE

That happened, yeah.

SAM

It probably really facilitated the moving-in process. Did you immediately scope out every place you went to, for someone likely?

TOM

Hey, Sam, Dee-Dee doesn't need to be interrogated by you.

SAM

I'm sure she doesn't.

DEE-DEE

I moved in with people. What's the big deal? I walk up to strangers and I start talking to them. I've always been that way. Sometimes one thing led to another. I'm older now and not so into that, but, you know—what's the big deal?

SAM

I guess I'm just a little more uptight than that.

DEE-DEE

Well—yeah. I guess so.

SAM

So, tell me what the—

TOM

Hey, listen, Sam, that's enough.

SAM

What?

TOM

Stop pestering her about her old boyfriends! Obviously she wouldn't want to talk about them in front of me.

DEE-DEE

I don't care. I have nothing to hide.

TOM

Well, *I* don't necessarily want to hear about them.

SAM

That's a rare and admirable quality. To have come this far in life and not have anything to hide.

DEE-DEE

No. It's not about what you've done. It's just about your attitude towards it.

SAM

Huh. Well, I wasn't going to ask you about your exes, anyway ... and, by the way, I hope I haven't offended you....

DEE-DEE

Oh, you haven't offended me.

SAM

Because I didn't mean to pry....

DEE-DEE

Like I said, I don't care. I don't have any big secrets or anything.

SAM

Well, I'm just curious about.... I mean, all that time you spent on the road, moving from one place to the other. What was the point of it? Do you feel like you accomplished anything from it? Or is it more like wasted time, that you regret not being able to get back?

DEE-DEE

SureI accomplished stuff. Or, well, I guess I didn't *accomplish* much. But I *gained* stuff.

SAM

You gained stuff.

DEE-DEE

Yeah. I don't know if Tom told you, but I'm a writer....

SAM

He told me, yeah.

DEE-DEE

Yeah. Well, I feel like I gained a lot of experience during those years. I mean, I kind of got an idea of how big the world is. And also how small. Of what people will do. Of all the crazy shit that goes on.

SAM

And you feel like all this is experience that you can use, now that you've settled down and can sort of take a long breather.

DEE-DEE

Exactly.

SAM

It sounds wonderful. To be able to move out here, live in the mountains, concentrate on school and your writing, for ... what? A few years, I guess—right?

DEE-DEE

Well. Yeah, I guess so. I mean, college is four years, right?

SAM

Traditionally, yes. And it'll be a busy four years for you,

what with writing, and school, and working. Do you work full-time?

DEE-DEE

Well....

TOM

We're thinking that Dee-Dee will just use this time to concentrate on her studies, Sam, and on her writing.

SAM

Well, of course she'll *concentrate* on that. But this is a big house, and there's still the mortgage to be paid.

DEE-DEE

Uh, actually, Tom—

TOM

My sister probably forgot that I already told her that I was going to take care of all the money stuff for the next few years, honey.

SAM

Wow. I guess I didn't realize that you were going to cover *everything*.

DEE-DEE

It's really amazing. I'm really grateful.

SAM

Yeah. Not a lot of people would do that.

DEE-DEE

I know they wouldn't.

SAM

What are you going to be working on? What writing project?

DEE-DEE

Oh, I haven't decided yet.

SAM

You mean you're still working out, like, the storyline, the subject matter, things like that.

DEE-DEE

Yeah. Pretty much.

SAM

What genre do you write?

DEE-DEE

Oh, I'm not sure.

SAM

No, I mean, are you working on a screenplay? A novel? A play? A book of short stories? Do you write poetry?

DEE-DEE

Yeah. I'm not sure.

SAM

Oh!... You're not sure about *that?*

DEE-DEE

I mean, I've kind of dabbled in all that stuff before, I've tried all of it. But I haven't really decided what my concentration should be. That's part of what's so great about Tom helping me out like this. Is that it'll give me a chance to sort of, you know, decide what I should do.

SAM

Uh-huh.... And Tom, you must really believe in Dee-Dee's writing to support her like this. You've read it, right?

TOM

Yeah, Sam, I have read it.

SAM

That's great.

TOM

Yeah. And *she's* great. Her writing's great.

SAM

That's wonderful.... But, Dee-Dee, you must have some leanings one way or the other, right?

DEE-DEE

I guess I would like to write a screenplay. But I think it's hard to get movies made. So maybe fiction would be better.

SAM

It's pretty hard to break into that market, too. Or even to get published by people who don't pay you anything at all.

DEE-DEE

I know that.

SAM

You really are so lucky to have someone like Tom, who's willing to be your patron. Usually people don't have that. They slave away for years, doing their real work during whatever little snatches of time they can steal from the jobs that keep them alive. Then, sometimes, *after* they've honed their craft, they get the chance to just do that and nothing else. But even then it's rare.

DEE-DEE

I know that. I know I'm lucky. Like I said, I'm thankful.

SAM

And of course, it takes more than just opportunity. Sometimes you assume that you have that creative spark, but then when you get out there and finally try to actually do something with it, you find out that you were wrong.

DEE-DEE

Is that what happened to you?

SAM

I guess in the end it's about what happens in the moment itself. Right? You can say you're anything you like, but there's no telling what the truth is until you show it by your actions.

DEE-DEE

I guess that's true.

SAM

You never know what you really are until you go out there and give it a shot. Have you done that yet? Like, have you actually *completed* anything? Or done anything hard? Have you finished any books, plays? Or have you ever tried making, say, a film?

DEE-DEE

A film?

SAM

Yeah. Have you ever made a film, Dee-Dee? Like, movies.

DEE-DEE

Why do you ask?

SAM

Why do I ask? Because apparently you're going to devote your life to it now....

DEE-DEE

No, I mean I just told you I hadn't really done anything like that before, that the whole reason I'm grateful to Tom is that he's letting me have the chance to really try....

SAM

Ah. *That's* the whole reason you're happy to be with Tom?

TOM

Okay, ladies. Dee-Dee, I'm sorry, I should have warned you about my little sister. When we were growing up she watched me getting away with everything while she wasn't allowed to ever get away with anything, and so she started taking upon herself the job of keeping me in line. Now it's a habit she can't seem to break, and not just with me.

SAM

My big brother likes to psychoanalyze me as a way of shutting me up.

DEE-DEE

I didn't mean to make you guys fight.

TOM

No, I'm telling you, we always fight. That's what we do. We have a miserable relationship. But we'll make an effort to be good.... Right, Sam?

SAM

Right. Yes—of course. Sorry, Dee-Dee. I can be a little ornery.

DEE-DEE

That's all right....Why did Tom get away with stuff when you didn't? I thought usually it was supposed to be the younger siblings who get away with stuff.

SAM

Because Tom was a boy.

TOM

Pretty much, yeah.

SAM

And as a girl I was held to a much higher standard. But

there was no pleasing Mom and Dad even when I did meet that standard. Because it was taken for granted that nothing I did could possibly be worth much, precisely because I was a girl.

DEE-DEE

Wow. I mean, like—in this day and age?

TOM

Sam's exaggerating a little bit. But, yeah, basically that's how it was.

DEE-DEE

That's terrible. I guess I didn't realize things were like that when you were growing up.

SAM

What do you mean?

DEE-DEE

Like, for your generation.

SAM

Ah.

TOM

Um, it was more like our family itself was weird, honey. It wasn't so much a generational thing.

SAM

Well, now, Tom, let's not forget that she is quite a bit younger than us. Like we were saying before. But I don't think things are better for your generation, Dee-Dee. In fact, it seems to me they're worse. I mean, as far as I can tell your generation has created a basically pornographic world for itself. It's really shocking, the way young women act nowadays. Not just pop stars, but ordinary women. It's like they take for granted that they should have all this respect and equality that was gained for them, by the efforts of women who came before. But then they behave more sluttishly than any generation of women probably ever has done, in all of history.

DEE-DEE

In all of history?

SAM

Like those girls in those "Girls Gone Wild" videos, for example.

TOM

Sam, I don't know that "Girls Gone Wild" is a fair representation of every woman Dee-Dee's age.

SAM

Seems to be pretty spot-on. At least, as far as a certain class of women goes, that is.

DEE-DEE

What class is that?

SAM

There seems to be a certain kind of young woman these days who gets by on her sex appeal. Who sort of attaches herself to men that are big enough suckers to take care of her. Which is fine, if you don't have your sights set any higher. But nowadays these girls also want to be taken seriously, as legitimate people. As artists, or whatever. It's like they don't quite get it, that using the basest parts of themselves in such a crude, manipulative way precludes them being taken seriously as real people.

(Pause.)

TOM

Dee-Dee, honey, I'm sorry. Sam and I have started fighting, and apparently she's too much of a bitch not to take it out on you.

DEE-DEE

Oh, so it's that obvious that she's talking about me?

SAM

I guess maybe you sort of reminded me in a way of those girls. Sorry—women. I wasn't thinking consciously of any connection, though.

TOM

Sam—I don't know. I think maybe I need to ask you to get a hotel room. I'm not sure you can stay with us, after all.

DEE-DEE

No, she can stay.

TOM

Honey—

DEE-DEE

I *want* her to stay.

SAM

Well, technically it's not your house, so if my brother wants to kick me out....

TOM

Dee-Dee. Partly it's that I should defend you against having to put up with this shit. But also—I mean, it's not exactly unheard-of for my sister and I to suddenly realize we can't be in the same room together.

SAM

The one redeeming quality of our relationship, Dee-Dee, is how open we are with each other. Even about the less savory parts of ourselves.

TOM

Pathologically open. Open as a wound.

DEE-DEE

You guys aren't open with each other at all. You just are going at each other's throats. I don't think that's very open. And maybe you're right, Tom. Maybe your sister should go, after all. I'm sorry, but I don't think she has a very good effect on you. You're kind of acting the way she does.

SAM

What could be worse than that?... Hey, listen. All right. I have issues. Okay? I have issues. And I'm a little stressed out, because I'm worried about my brother. I'm worried about whether or not he knows what he's doing, know what I mean? No offense, or anything. I was so worried about him that I flew all the way out here. And, let's be honest, if you think about it you'll agree that my worries are at least a little justified, right? Am I right? But maybe I did go a little too far. I always go too far. Tom can tell you. But my heart's in the right place. Usually.

TOM

It's true, she does go too far. And it's true that her heart is in the vicinity of the right place. Sometimes.

SAM

Thank you.

TOM

Or, well, maybe not the "right" place. Maybe just an "okay" place.

DEE-DEE

It's okay, Sam. Tom warned me that you were fucked up.

SAM

That was nice of him.

TOM

I had a feeling it might wind up being necessary.

SAM

And here I thought you were filled with all these beautiful high hopes for my visit.

TOM

Hope for the best, prepare for the worst.

DEE-DEE

I thought he was exaggerating.

SAM

Well, now you know the truth. I'd still like to have some girl talk, if we're going to be sisters. I'd like to hear more of the details of this big crazy life you've had. But in the meantime I'll be happy to get a hotel room. Even if we had gotten off on the right foot, I'd hate to feel like I was imposing.

DEE-DEE

No. I want you to stay.

TOM

Yeah, well....

DEE-DEE

Let's keep her here. Please, baby.

TOM

All right. It's up to Sam. And to you.

DEE-DEE

Thank you, sweetie.

(Dee-Dee kisses Tom as Sam watches coldly.)

TOM

Okay, baby. Listen, do me a favor. Let me talk to my sister alone for a little bit. Okay?

SAM

I won't hurt him.

DEE-DEE

All right. I'll go get the laundry started and then we can go to dinner later on.

(teasingly, as she puts in her iPod earbuds:)

And I'll have my music on. So you guys can be as "open" as you want, and don't mind me.

(Exit Dee-Dee.)

TOM

You flew all the way out here to fuck up my life and boss me around.

SAM

I flew out here to help you.

TOM

I can't trust you, Sam. Do you understand that? Because you just got done saying you would be on your best behavior. I mean, was that your best behavior?

SAM

Fuck that. I was all set to be nice to her. But then.... God! Just the way she was talking!

TOM

What was wrong with how she talked?

SAM

I'm telling you, Tom. There's things you don't know about her.

TOM

Cut that shit out.

SAM

Specific things.

TOM

If you have something to say, Sam, then just say it. Or, actually, you know what? *Don't* say it.

SAM

It's something that I flew all the way from New York to tell you.

TOM

I don't give a damn about whether it inconvenienced you to come out here, I'm telling you I don't want to hear it.

SAM

You mean to tell me that you could stand to know that I have some fact about Dee-Dee, some little secret, without ever asking me what it is?

TOM

That's right.

SAM

Wow. I'm impressed. That's willpower.

TOM

Not at all. I just trust Dee-Dee.

SAM

Great

(Pause.)

TOM

Anyway, how could you have found out so much about Dee-Dee?

SAM

Just did.

TOM

What did you do, hire a private eye?

SAM

No. Just lucked into it.

TOM

What does that mean?

SAM

You remember that guy I was dating last? Wally?

TOM

Yeah. Sorry that didn't work out, Sam.

SAM

Yeah, well.... Nothing new, you know?

TOM

Yeah, I know. But the last time we saw each other.... Anyway, I know you had big hopes for that guy. And it seemed like things were going well. I know you're under a lot of stress still from having just broken up with him.

SAM

Yeah, well. There were lots of things about ol' Wally that I didn't feel obligated to tell you that maybe made him a little less than perfect. Like, he had a big thing for internet porn.

TOM

Oh, well, that's not such a big deal.

SAM

Typical male response.

TOM

Uh, yeah—that's my whole point. It's a typically male thing. Lots of guys watch porn on the internet.

SAM

Okay, well, I don't necessarily want to know whether or not my big brother is spending a lot of free time watching young strangers hump on his computer....

TOM

Hey, newsflash: *I am.* So is every male with internet access you know. It's not the classiest fact of life, maybe, but it's pretty harmless.

SAM

So I guess what you're saying is that it's my fault Wally and I broke up. Because I'm such a priggish bitch.

TOM

No. That's not what I meant.... Was that why you guys broke up, Sam? Did you leave him because he watched internet porn?

SAM

No. Obviously not. I mean, I'm past the point of expecting *miraculous* standards, you know. There was plenty of other stuff.

TOM

Okay.

SAM

But the porn.... I used his laptop once, towards the end. I started to type in the navigation bar, and all his favorites scrolled down. And, I mean, you should have seen this shit. It wasn't just ... *normal* stuff. I mean, it was *filthy.*

TOM

Filthy how?

SAM

I don't want to talk about it, okay?

TOM

Sure, sure.

SAM

I clicked on one of the sites....

TOM

Oh, *really?*

SAM

Because of Wally, not because I wanted to get off. I wanted to see what it was that was so fascinating to him. So I clicked on the first u.r.l., the top one in his scroll of favorites. And I looked at it, and it was just ... I mean, those girls—they're kids. They're just so young, they're children.

TOM

Wait, you mean, Wally was into...?

SAM

No no no, they weren't minors, but they were young, they were just kids! I watched for a second, I couldn't stand to watch any longer, because I just kept thinking, "That's someone's daughter." I know that's a cliché, but that's what I was thinking.

TOM

There's usually someone's son involved, too.

SAM

Yeah, well—and hey, don't make fun of me.

TOM

I wasn't making fun, necessarily. I was making *light* of it. But I wasn't making *fun* of it.

SAM

I watched.... I mean, there's nothing wrong with giving blow jobs, or with doing it in weird positions, or any of that stuff. I know there isn't. But to do it in public! Where anybody can see! I was watching this one video, and I kept thinking, What would her family say? What would her poor mom say, her poor dad say? Her poor boyfriend say?

TOM

Well, Sam, they might not mind as much as you think they would.

SAM

Oh, that's what you think, huh?

TOM

How many times did you watch this one particular video, Sam?

SAM

I did watch it more than once, actually.

TOM

You watched it more than once. Listen. I remember how you used to take it to heart, all Mom and Dad's weird fundamentalist stuff. It always got to you worse than it did to me—I guess probably because you were the girl. Do you remember that thing with that dumb Harlequin romance novel?

SAM

No.

TOM

Oh, come on.

SAM

Oh, all right, fine.

TOM

Mom said they were basically pornography and that you were forbidden to read them. Man, that just blew me away, because I always thought Harlequin romance novels were just the dorkiest, girliest things ever. I used to make fun of you for reading them.

SAM

Yes, I know you did.

TOM

But after Mom declared them off-limits I started sneaking peeks at them myself.

SAM

What did you think?

TOM

Some pretty hot stuff! But you remember the time I'm talking about, though. When Dad caught you with that romance novel?

SAM

It was only a couple days after Mom made up that rule. I would have minded her—I mean, it was a stupid rule, but that never stopped me. But I was still right in the middle of that one book. I wasn't trying to rebel or anything. I just figured that obviously the new rule shouldn't take effect until after I'd gotten done with that one book.

TOM

And then Dad caught you with it....

SAM

The thing was, he didn't even care about that stupid rule.

His opinion of Harlequin romance novels was about the same as yours. Even he thought Mom was being over-dramatic on that one. But I guess when he caught me reading it, he saw his chance to teach me a lesson about defying parental authority.

TOM

I guess so.... Go on.

SAM

Jesus Christ, are you kidding? You were sitting right there for the whole thing.

TOM

Yeah, I know, but I don't think it would hurt you to sort of, you know....

SAM

Relive it?

TOM

That's not the term I would use.

SAM

It's not like this is some buried trauma I've been blocking for years, you know.... Anyway. Fine. He saw me reading that stupid book and he freaked out. It was—Jesus. It was *Pirate,* by Fabio.

TOM

By Fabio?

SAM

Allegedly by Fabio. Or no, not even allegedly. I mean, on the acknowledgements page Fabio wrote a big thank-you to his ghost writer, so, you know, I mean, that's real transparency. Anyway. I just wanted to know what happened to the pirates. To me it was a book about pirates—sexy pirates, but, still, pirates—and I wanted to find out what happened to them. But Dad caught me reading it in my bedroom and he just blew his top. He called me a little whore and dragged me out into the living room and made me stand before him in the middle of that room while he sat in his armchair, like a king on a throne, and he made me rip the book up while he watched.

TOM

You were twelve, right?

SAM

Right. And you were sitting next to him the whole time, watching TV. Just a couple of good ol' boys, hanging out.

TOM

I was *pretending* to watch TV, Sam.

SAM

Uh-huh. Pretty convincingly.

TOM

Jesus Christ. I was a kid, too. What was I supposed to do?

SAM

Nothing. Never mind. Who cares. All I wanted was to find

out what happened to the pirates.... Anyway, you're the one who brought this up. Why are we even talking about it?

TOM

It's the kind of experience that never leaves you.

SAM

Particularly when people keep bringing it up.

TOM

Sam, listen—all I'm trying to say is, you have some hang-ups about sex. Which is to be expected, considering the way things were. Which is nothing to be ashamed of. But which should be taken into account.

SAM

Um. I think that what you describe as "hang-ups," another person might call "moderately traditional views," but, hey, whatever.... Under exactly which circumstances do you think I should be taking these hang-ups into account?

TOM

I think there's some projection going on here.

SAM

Projection.

TOM

All I mean is that maybe some of the feelings of disgust you feel about the girls in those videos are feelings that you're afraid other people would have toward you, if they ever caught on to your desires.

SAM

Do you think that I have the desire to be in an internet porn video?

TOM

All I'm saying is that the fact that these girls are in these videos ... well, it's probably not as tragic as you think.

SAM

Dee-Dee was in it.

TOM

I beg your pardon?

SAM

That video that I kept watching. The reason I kept watching was to make sure that it really was Dee-Dee who was in it. Not because of some hare-brained Freudian reason.

TOM

What are you talking about?

SAM

Your "fiancée." Yeah, good idea about not signing a pre-nup. There probably aren't any nasty surprises lurking in her bio, or anything.

TOM

This isn't funny.

SAM

Agreed.

TOM

I'm serious.

SAM

Me too. I'm so serious, I flew all the way out here from New York.

TOM

What fucking bullshit. You wouldn't have been able to recognize her. You hadn't even met her before she walked in the door.

SAM

Jesus, Tom, I've seen her in your Facebook albums. And besides, is that the best you can do? Your immediate response is not, "My Dee-Dee would never fuck strangers for money, post the video on the internet, and then not tell me and just wait until one of my buddies who'd stumbled upon it took pity on me and filled me in"? The only thing about what I just said that strikes you as implausible is that I would have recognized Dee-Dee?

TOM

I swear to Christ, Sam, you've gone too far this time. I am gonna knock you on your fucking ass.

SAM

Now we're getting somewhere.

TOM

I'm serious.

SAM

Wait. Are you projecting?

TOM

You've gone too far.

SAM

I'm telling the truth.

TOM

Bullshit. You just happened upon the one video that has my Dee-Dee in it, during the one time in your tight-ass life you ever watched a porno? Yeah, right.

SAM

Maybe it's not "the one video" that she's made. Maybe she's done so many thousands that any time you click on a porno, the odds are good that you'll end up watching her.

TOM

I am gonna punch you in the mouth, Sam.

SAM

If you don't believe me then what are you so angry about?

TOM

Because you are disrespecting the woman I love! Now shut your mouth and pack your shit.

SAM

Why don't you let me prove it to you?

TOM

Because you can't prove it to me, because it isn't true. Now come on, get your stuff.

SAM

I brought my laptop.

TOM

Fuck you.

SAM

It's already unpacked and everything.

TOM

Fuck off.

SAM

Let me show you.

TOM

No. There's nothing to show. And even just going along with you for a second, even just humoring you, would be disrespectful to Dee-Dee.

SAM

Oh my God, come off it, big brother. It's nothing to be ashamed of, remember? You just got done saying so yourself, that only a neurotic like me would be upset by that stuff. Besides, we both know that the only *real* reason you could possibly have not to let me show you this website is that you figure I'm telling the truth.

(Pause.)

TOM

All right. Show me what you're talking about.

(They sit. Sam gets her laptop out, sets it up.)

I don't believe you. But even if it turned out that what you're saying is true, you're right. It wouldn't matter.

SAM

Really. It wouldn't even matter that she'd kept it hidden from you?

TOM

Like I said earlier—people have a right to their secrets.

SAM

Well. She's a lucky girl to have such an understanding boyfriend. Should we watch this with the volume on? Or would that disturb Dee-Dee?

TOM

Mute it.

(They watch the video for about forty seconds. They are seated facing us and the laptop screen is facing away from the audience.)

Turn it off, please.

(Sam stops the video. Pause.)

You've finally done it. You've ruined my life.

SAM

Oh, come on.

TOM

You've ruined my life.

SAM

I had to tell you, Tom. You needed to know. Can you imagine if I'd stumbled upon that video, and then *not* told you about it? What kind of person would I be then, huh?

TOM

You've ruined my life.

SAM

Stop saying that.

TOM

I can't believe you showed me this.

SAM

Tom. I'm asking you, how could I not have showed you this?

TOM

You just had to do it, didn't you?

SAM

Uh, yes. I did have to do it.

TOM

What did you do, did you, did you investigate her? Did you go nosing around in her past?

SAM

What? I told you, Tom, I just happened upon it.

TOM

You probably went and hired a private investigator. The minute I told you I'd found someone. You just couldn't stand it.

SAM

Hey, you're goddam right, I couldn't stand it. Now this is very cute, your turning this shit around on me, but it's not going to fly, big brother. Not this time.

TOM

I feel like I've been poisoned.

SAM

You *have* been, big brother. You *have* been. But is it my fault? Did I do it?

TOM

Yes.

SAM

Your little Dee-Dee is the one doing the nasty for the camera. Hey, she needed some way to fund all her big adventures, right? And I guess this beat working. But don't worry, now she's moving on. Now she's graduated to *you.* Congratulations. Aren't you proud?

TOM

Yes. I am proud.

SAM

Oh, wow.

TOM

I love her.

SAM

Fine. Love away, if you can manage it. I've done all I can do. You want to know what me finding that website was? *A lucky break.*

TOM

Yeah. For you.

SAM

Fine. Fine, big brother.

TOM

Listen. When Dee-Dee comes back in here, don't you mention any of this to her.

SAM

It's not my job to mention it.

TOM

Nobody's mentioning any of this to her. Not ever.

SAM

Up to you. Although that'll be quite a feat.

(Enter Dee-Dee.)

DEE-DEE

Hey.

SAM

Hello there.

TOM

Hey.

DEE-DEE

I'm getting hungry. Do you guys think you'll be ready to eat soon?

TOM

I don't know, babe. I can't really drive right now.

DEE-DEE

What?

TOM

Plus I don't really have an appetite.

DEE-DEE

What's going on?

TOM

Nothing. Just sit with us a while.

DEE-DEE

Did something happen?

TOM

No, just sit.

DEE-DEE

All right.

TOM

Tell us about what you're working on, Dee-Dee.

DEE-DEE

What?

TOM

About what you're writing.

DEE-DEE

You're gonna start quizzing me too, huh?

TOM

No! No, I'm just curious.

DEE-DEE

You just happen to all of a sudden be so curious about what I'm writing.

SAM

Well, what's wrong with that? Doesn't he have a right to just be curious?

DEE-DEE

Because he's paying for it, you mean.

SAM

Well, no, I just mean because he's your boyfriend....

TOM

I didn't mean to quiz you, sweetie, I just meant—because I'm curious.

DEE-DEE

All of a sudden.

TOM

Not all of a sudden. I'm talking about it all of a sudden,

but that doesn't mean I haven't thought about it. It's just that before, I....You know that I used to want to be a writer? Sure you do, I guess. At least, I've told you before that I used to write stuff occasionally. Although I guess practically everyone who can read and write has kind of wanted to be a writer. Anyway. It always bugged me that I hadn't done enough. I felt like I hadn't had enough experiences, like I hadn't earned the right to think of myself as a writer. I felt like I would be able to be an artist someday, in the future, after I'd paid some dues by going out and having adventures. And I always felt ashamed of myself because I never got around to having those adventures.

DEE-DEE

Well, but everyone has experiences. You can't help it, even if sometimes you would like to. Everyone has material.

TOM

Yeah, I know you're right. But you know what I mean, too, don't you?

SAM

I think what my brother is asking is if that's why you left home and went off into the big bad world and did whatever it was you did. Was so you could gather up experience and material for later.

TOM

I'm not asking if that's why she did it, I'm saying that I, you know, I understand that that's why....

DEE-DEE

You "understand"?... Uh, okay. I guess partly that was

why. But not mainly. Mainly was that I wanted to learn about the world. I lived in kind of a small place where it felt like nothing was going on and I wanted to see if there was crazy stuff happening in other places. And there totally was. Probably there was at home, too, if I'd looked and not been so set on leaving. But now I'm done. I get it. I'm ready to, you know, to stop. Settle down. Focus on things that are a little less superficial.... Okay?

TOM

Okay. Sure.
(Pause.)
Crazy stuff, huh?

DEE-DEE

What?

TOM

You found crazy stuff, huh?

DEE-DEE

Yeah. That's what I said. Honey, I.... So, Sam, you never did that?

SAM

I beg your pardon?

DEE-DEE

You seem to think it's so weird of me to have gone off to like find myself—

SAM

Find yourself!

DEE-DEE

—so I assume you never did anything wild and crazy like that. Right? You just sort of stayed home. Did what was expected.

SAM

To be honest I was never clear on what I was expected to do....

DEE-DEE

Whatever you were told, I guess.

SAM

I must strike you as pretty tame. But as my brother can attest, I have not turned out like my parents wanted. At least they've never seemed particularly satisfied with me.

TOM

That's true. Normally I would add "through no fault of her own," but today, I don't know, I'm beginning to see their point.

DEE-DEE

Can I tell you guys something?

TOM

What is it, sweetie?

DEE-DEE

What's going on?

SAM

See, darling, that's a question, so technically that would be "asking" us something. "Telling us something" would be if you were to make some sort of a statement.

TOM

Hey, watch how you talk to her in my house, you fucking cunt!

DEE-DEE

What?!

TOM

Dee-Dee, baby, I'm sorry. Sam'll apologize or else we'll politely ask her to get the fuck out of here....

DEE-DEE

No! *What* did you call her?!

TOM

Uh ... Sam?

SAM.

She means "cunt," Tom. Dee-Dee, "cunt" is a word that men sometimes use. You must have heard it before.

TOM

Oh ... sorry, honey....

DEE-DEE

"Sorry"? You're "sorry"?

TOM

Yeah, that's right! I'm sorry!

DEE-DEE

I hate that word, Tom!

TOM

Well, I didn't call you it!

DEE-DEE

This is exactly what I was going to say earlier. Was that I don't like this whole vibe between you two.

SAM

"Vibe"?

TOM

Look, Dee-Dee, my sister and I have a stormy relationship....

SAM

Has your generation brought the word "vibe" back into circulation?

TOM

Hey, fucking can it about the whole age thing, you fucking bitch!

DEE-DEE

Tom, I don't like words like that!

TOM

Like what?

SAM.

Like "vibe."

TOM

I swear to fucking God....

DEE-DEE

Tom! You are scaring me!

TOM

I'm sorry, baby. I'll try to calm down.

DEE-DEE

What is going on here, anyway?

TOM

Just a good old-fashioned family reunion, sweetie.

DEE-DEE

You're a whole different person around her.

TOM

It's true. I should have warned you, I guess. From experience you would think I'd know to, by now. But I always assume that it's going to be different. I can't even call it a "hope," it really is just an assumption. Because I say to myself every time, "Of course Sam and I won't rip each other's guts out this time. Why would we? There's no reason for us *not* to be decent to each other, so obviously we will be decent." Believe it or not, I somehow manage to forget that there never has been any reason for us to hurt each other, and yet that hasn't stopped us ever in our whole lives.

SAM

Why do you suppose that is, big brother?

TOM

Because we're a couple of stupid wild animals, I assume.

DEE-DEE

I feel like there's something going on.

TOM

There's a whole big complicated history between us.

DEE-DEE

There's something you're not telling me.

SAM

Part of what he's not telling you is that whole big complicated history we were just referring to. Which, believe me, would take a long time to fill you in on.

TOM

It's actually not all that complicated. It's just this, over and over again.

DEE-DEE

He's changed, since you got here. What did you do?

SAM

Excuse me?

DEE-DEE

What did you do to Tom? He was already in a bad mood when I left the room a few minutes ago, but not like this. You must have done something to him.

SAM

Just had a conversation.

TOM

All right, hey, that's enough.

DEE-DEE

Why?

TOM

Because just, hey, you know, let's cool down. You know?

DEE-DEE

I am cool, I'm just asking a question is all.

TOM

Well, let's change the subject....

DEE-DEE

What, I'm supposed to just suddenly forget that you've started using the c-word all of a sudden?

TOM

I'm sorry I used that word, honey. I really am. But that's all the more reason for us to, you know, steer the conversation in another direction.

DEE-DEE

No, it's all the more reason for you to tell me what's going on so that I can understand how this big transformation happened.

TOM

Oh, Jesus, listen, there's no transformation, I just happened to use a bad word is all, I'm sorry.

DEE-DEE

Tell me what happened.

TOM

No.

DEE-DEE

So something did happen.

TOM

Never mind.

DEE-DEE

Sam, could me and Tom talk alone a minute?

TOM

Her leaving won't make any difference.

DEE-DEE

You won't tell me, no matter what.

TOM

There's nothing to tell.

DEE-DEE

I know there is.

TOM

Well. Either way.

DEE-DEE

Something's changed. I can feel it.

SAM

That's a vibe.

DEE-DEE

Why do you have to provoke me like that? Why does it have to be everyone against everyone? Shouldn't *someone* be on *someone's* side? *(to Tom:)* Either you and me, because we love each other and we're going to get married. *(to Sam:)* Or you and me, because of the way he's been talking about women.

TOM

What?

DEE-DEE

You using the c-word. And "bitch."

TOM

I am sorry I said the c-word. But "bitch," I mean—is that really so bad? I just always think of it as the female form of "asshole." Like, "actor, actress," "asshole, bitch."

DEE-DEE

I don't like it.

TOM

Okay. I won't do it anymore.

DEE-DEE

It isn't like you.

TOM

No. I'd like to think it isn't, at least.

DEE-DEE

Are you going to tell me what was going on between you two? While I was out of the room?

TOM

Nothing went on.

DEE-DEE

If she weren't here would you tell me?

TOM

There's nothing to tell.

DEE-DEE

Okay. Fine. Great. I guess I just wish you could be honest with me.

TOM

Excuse me?

DEE-DEE

I said I guess I wish I could just count on you to be open with me about everything, the way I always thought I could before now, and the way I try to be with you.

TOM

Well. You *can* count on me. And now I suggest we drop it.

SAM

So, Dee-Dee, you feel like a couple should tell each other everything? Everything important, I mean—I guess there isn't time to tell *everything*.

DEE-DEE

You're mocking me. But yeah, that is what I believe.

SAM

So if you, for example—

TOM

Sam, I am going to physically beat the fucking shit out of you if you don't cut it out.

DEE-DEE

Hey! I don't like that!

TOM

I don't like it either!

DEE-DEE

Okay, fine! I'm glad to find out that when your sister's around you turn into a totally secretive asshole! Or maybe you've always been one and now it's just that the truth comes out!

(Dee-Dee starts to exit.)

TOM

Hey, Dee-Dee!

(Dee-Dee stops.)

DEE-DEE

Yeah?

TOM

It's true. There is a secret between us.

DEE-DEE

There is?

TOM

Yeah. It's the kind of thing that ... well, some people would call it a deep, dark secret. In fact, it's so.... I don't know if it should come out or not.

DEE-DEE

Well, now it has to.

TOM

I guess it does. Yeah. But we can.... I mean, I feel like, whatever happens, whatever skeletons we have in our closets, we can get over them. Right?

DEE-DEE

Well. Depends what it is.

TOM

Depends what it is?

DEE-DEE

Yeah. I mean, if you want me to say that I would, like, totally unconditionally forgive anything that you ever did, well, I can't say that for sure. Some things I wouldn't forgive.

TOM

Got it. So then I guess the reverse is true, too. I'd prefer to think it wasn't, but I guess.... So there are things you might do, that you wouldn't expect me to ever forgive. That you would want to hide from me. At all costs.

DEE-DEE

Hypothetically. But there isn't anything like that.

TOM

No?

DEE-DEE

Of course not.

TOM

Because, if there was, maybe you would be surprised at how much I could forgive. Because you're very important to me, Dee-Dee. You're very, extremely important. And if there were something in your past, I would want to find a way to forgive you.

DEE-DEE

Yeah, well, there isn't. So if you're looking for any of that Q.E.D. action, you're out of luck.

TOM

Sorry, Q.E.D.?

DEE-DEE

You know. That Latin or Greek or whatever thing. Like, you give me something, I give you something.

TOM.

Oh. Uh, honey, that's not "Q.E.D.," that's, uh—

SAM

"Quid pro quo."

TOM

Yeah. "Quid pro quo."

DEE-DEE

All right, fine. Q.E.D., quid pro quo, whatever. Anyway. The point is, I wish you would just man up and confess to whatever it is you have to tell me.

TOM

Man up, huh.

DEE-DEE

Yeah. Man up.

TOM

Man up. You want me to act like a man, I guess. You want me to act like a regular man.

DEE-DEE

I want you to act like a grown-up and just tell me whatever you're going to tell me and shake off whatever mind control your sister is using on you.

TOM

It's interesting. It's interesting that you don't think you'd be able to forgive me for anything, unconditionally.

DEE-DEE

No one can promise that. Why should I be able to?

TOM

The reason it's good to be able to promise unconditional forgiveness is because then the other person might feel called upon to promise the same thing. If something ever came up. Quid pro quo. Like if, say, hypothetically, it came out that you had used to be a porn star.

(Pause.)

DEE-DEE

That would be something that needed forgiving?

SAM

Wow, that's not what I was expecting her to say....

TOM

Okay, you know what, Sam? Why don't you take off a while. Your little job here is finished.

SAM

I think you're right. I'll just take a stroll around the neighborhood....

DEE-DEE

What, this is why you came all the way out here? Not to get to know me at all. To tattle on me?

SAM

I came out here to tell my brother what I knew about you, yes.

DEE-DEE

And you had to come all the way out in person and do it, of course, you couldn't just tell him over the phone or in an e-mail, you wanted to be here so you could rubberneck at this big, like, train wreck you've set up.

SAM

Uh, it's not exactly the sort of thing you tell someone over the phone. You want to be able to let them know in person. When it's someone you love.

DEE-DEE

Oh, because you're so fucking loving. Anyway. The show's started, take your seat or whatever.

TOM

This doesn't have anything to do with her.

DEE-DEE

Are you fucking kidding me? How would you even have found out, if it weren't for this, this bitch, snooping around, having me checked out?

TOM

Right. The, uh, the *circumstances* have to do with her. That's true. I never would have found out about the porn stuff if it weren't for Sam, I guess, since, I mean, clearly you weren't going to tell me. But the fundamental issue, the fact that you used to do porno, that has nothing to do with Sam. That's between us.

DEE-DEE

It is, huh?... So you think I should have told you about all that, then?

TOM

Yeah, I do.

DEE-DEE

Why?

TOM

Because I think that I have a right to know that you used to do that.

DEE-DEE

"Used to"? What makes you think I don't still do it?

TOM

All right, now. That isn't funny.

DEE-DEE

How do you know?

TOM

Because you don't need to anymore.

DEE-DEE

Oh, yeah? That's interesting. Exactly what need is it that you think I was fulfilling then, that I don't have anymore?

TOM

Um. Money, I guess.

DEE-DEE

Oh, and now you've bought me.

TOM

That does seem to be the way to get you.... I'm sorry, I didn't, uh....

DEE-DEE

What if there was some other need? Huh? A need I still have? That can only be satisfied by being dirty and going out and making these little movies. That you couldn't buy off. What then, huh?

TOM

Okay, you need to not goad me, all right, because.... Sam, why did you show me that?

SAM

Oh, Tom, I had to, is all.

TOM

I have such an empty life. I have such a.... I wish you hadn't shown me that.

DEE-DEE

Don't be upset, baby. I was only fooling with you, about still doing it. I mean, of course I, you know, I would never sleep with anybody else, when I'm with you. Unless we talked about it first. I just ... that was a long time ago, is all.

SAM

It couldn't have been that long ago. You're not old enough.

TOM

Why did you do it, Dee-Dee? Was it the money?

DEE-DEE

Yeah, sure, it was mainly the money.

TOM

Were you—did someone force you?

DEE-DEE

(laughing)

No!

TOM

Well, there must have been something! You could have gotten a job anywhere—

DEE-DEE

Where?!

TOM

Anywhere! McDonald's, Wal-Mart....

DEE-DEE

Oh, Jesus. Hey, if I'm going to sell myself, I would like to at least get paid decent.

SAM

Is that a pun? "Decent"?

TOM

For the last time, Sam, you leave her alone. Just because she may not ... she may not be....

(Tom starts to cry.)

DEE-DEE

Tom ... Tom ... don't cry ... why are you crying?... It's true, I did keep it from you. But not because I'm ashamed of it. But just, I figured you wouldn't understand.

TOM

Explain it, then.

DEE-DEE.

Explain it? I'd just gotten to Miami. I didn't have any money, and I didn't know anyone. I was at a club and I started letting these guys buy me drinks and then they were like, "You wanna make some money?," and I was like, "Fuck you." But then they were so, like, professional and everything, and up-front, and I realized they were serious. Like, about it being a real business venture. And then ... well ... why not? It wasn't like I had a boyfriend at the time. And I, I guess I never imagined that people I knew would wind up seeing the videos.

TOM

I guess when you're sort of alone in the world you do all kinds of.... I hate to think of you like that, alone in Miami, penniless, no friends. In fucking Miami.

DEE-DEE

But, Tom—don't be sad. Nothing bad happened to me. I was there because I wanted to be. I needed money, and, you know, it was something I didn't, like, mind doing, anyway. It was just kind of, whatever. I mean, it's different now. We have this committed thing, so, you know, obviously now I would never ... but then....

TOM

Do you really expect this not to bother me?

DEE-DEE

I hope it won't bother you. I think it shouldn't bother you.

TOM

You are a fucking pornographer!

DEE-DEE

Was! Was a pornographer! Anyway, no, I don't see the big deal! Because, I mean, if you found out that I'd done all this same stuff in my past, but just without a video camera and money, then you'd be like, "Oh, well, the past is the past, and what you did then is your own business." So I don't see what the difference is! If you wanna know every crazy sexual thing I ever did in my whole life, I guess I'll tell you, because I have nothing to hide. So what's the difference if you find out because someone told you, or if you find out because someone videotaped it? It's the same thing.

SAM

Amazing. See, this is what I was saying before, about your generation. See, *it makes a difference* that there were cameras involved. Not to mention money. But let's just table the whole issue of your literally being a whore. Let's talk about the.... I mean, let's say you got freaky with half a dozen guys at once, one time in your college days—or, wait, sorry, you didn't have many college days—but anyway, let's say you did that, just for your own particular pleasure. Let's even say you videotaped it for your own weird personal whatever. I won't pretend not to be what I guess you'd call a prude, I won't pretend not to think that that's a total fucking travesty of human sexuality, but, hey, I am willing to admit that it's your business. But, I mean, are you capable of understanding that when you broadcast it over the internet, when you turn into one of those people that are so cheerfully polluting the whole culture with your dumb-ass filth, are you even able to comprehend that at that point, by definition, it is now everybody's business? It's *my* business, because it's *my* boyfriend who's watching you oh-so-professionally suck some cock that just popped out of your . . .

(she can't bring herself to finish the phrase)

. . .and I've got to lie there and know that he's thinking about you, you and your five or eight or however many dopey little friends, doing that, and wishing I would let him do that, too, and thinking about what a frigid bitch I am for not letting him.

DEE-DEE

Then you should ask him not to watch that stuff if it makes you feel bad. What has that got to do with me?

TOM

Like I said before, Sam, I don't think it's fair to make Dee-Dee this big representative of her whole generation. I'm starting to get the feeling that Dee-Dee here is a special case.

DEE-DEE

I thought you were going to be my sister.

SAM

Well, I'm not your fucking sister.

DEE-DEE.

Yeah, I know. But I thought you were going to be. I was excited about you. My new big sister. I mean, boo-hoo, right? But for real—I always felt all alone growing up.

I never had anyone to look after me. And now, I mean, I know I'm technically a grown-up and it's too late for anyone to take care of me, but still—I want it. And thinking about you coming, I was so excited, I felt like a little kid. And now it turns out.... I mean, you came all the way out here just to *get* me.

TOM

She came all the way out here to.... I mean, she's *my* sister. She came out here to look after *me.* To tell me this thing that you obviously were never gonna tell me.

DEE-DEE

Tom, I—all right, fine. Can we just, like, talk about it later?

TOM

Oh, sure, yeah. Why not? It's nothing important. Just the fact that I almost got married to a fucking whore.

DEE-DEE

Tom, don't say that.

TOM

Don't say what? "Whore"? You know, it would have been one thing if you'd shown the slightest emotion or regret. Not that I wanted to see you cry, but I was expecting you to and I was expecting to forgive you, because you were going to be sorry. But for you to be so cavalier about it. For you not to even see why I would be hurt by what you did. I take it back, you're not a whore. A whore is a human being who's been forced by circumstances into a shitty, degrading position. Who might still be capable of shame, even if she covers it up with some sort of bluster. But you, you're something new. Something worse. You're not even really a human being.

DEE-DEE

I.... Okay, look. I guess I can understand maybe why you're hurt....

TOM

Wow. I'm really proud of you for that.

DEE-DEE

Okay, you know, this is emotionally stressful and I understand that but you are being really mean to me right now! I mean it isn't like I betrayed you or anything, all right? I didn't even know you back then!

TOM

You're right. It's not the same thing as if you were the woman I loved, and you turned around and gave in to some disgusting urge, and then you came back to me and said you were sorry. Instead, it's like, I get to suddenly find out that the person I love isn't there at all. She has, like, no relation whatsoever to who I thought she was. She was just this pretty illusion that covered up this, this *hole,* this shallow nothingness that doesn't understand jack shit about the way normal human beings with feelings about each other live their lives.

DEE-DEE

You ... you say that to me? Is it really all that big of a shock that I would have done a porno?

SAM

Dee-Dee, hey. Maybe that isn't the best tack to take, honey.

DEE-DEE

I mean, a half-hour ago it was still sexy that I was this big crazy adventurous person who'd been all over the country and had done all this wild unpredictable shit, but now that you've gotten up close and seen what it actually entails, now all of a sudden you can't handle it.

TOM

I'm not going to dignify that with a response. You know why? Because the only appropriate response would be to beat the fucking shit out of you.

SAM

Okay, Tom, cool down. I know you're upset, but you're gonna wind up in a lot of trouble over this....

DEE-DEE

What! You actually believe he would really hit me?!

SAM

Honey, men hit women over this kind of stuff. Don't you know that?

DEE-DEE

Yeah, some men. Asshole men. But not nice men, like Tom....

TOM

Yeah. Nice guys like Tom. Pussy dickweeds that you can push around. Pathetic shitheads that are so incredibly lonely and needy that they'll let you do any fucking thing you want to them. Losers who don't mind taking whatever internet slag is left over.

SAM

Tom—hey, Tom, I know you're upset, but try to calm down—

TOM

Get the fuck out of my house! I mean get the fuck out of here!

DEE-DEE

Tom—sweetie—no....

TOM

Get the fuck out or I'll kill you!

DEE-DEE

Stop saying that! Why would you ever say that?! Even as a joke? Even when you're really mad? And where am I supposed to go, what am I supposed to do? I can't, I can't just wander off like I used to, I'm so tired of living like that....

TOM

The only joke around here is me. Now get the fuck out, I said. I know you don't have any money, I'll write you a check. I figure that with all the times you've fucked me, you've earned a pretty good chunk of change.

DEE-DEE

Oh, Tom....

SAM

Tom, hey ... you don't have to be....

TOM

Oh, you have got to be kidding me.

DEE-DEE

Don't pretend you don't watch it! I've seen your history

when I use your computer. I go up to the navigation bar and I type in www and I see what pops up. Pornrabbit dot com. Assparade dot com. College Fuck Fest dot com.

TOM

That's different!

DEE-DEE

How is it different?

SAM

Don't be ridiculous.

DEE-DEE

How is it different?

TOM

Because I, I *every once in a while,* if I'm feeling lonely....

DEE-DEE

Ha! Ha! Ha!

TOM

Or, fine, if I'm feeling *horny!* If I'm feeling horny then every once in a while I jerk off to a fucking internet video! In a moment of *weakness!* That's different from having it be my way of life, from having it be my livelihood!

DEE-DEE

You know what the difference is, between you and me? Is that you're a fucking pussy. And a hypocrite. Because you pretend to think it's so bad, when really you love it. But me, I don't hate it. And I don't love it. I don't feel anything about it, and I don't say anything about it. Not like you and your bitch sister, who use it to make yourselves think you're better than me.

TOM

No, you know what the difference is between you and me, really? The difference is that I am going to stay here and you are going to get the fuck out!

SAM

She's just a dumb kid is all, Tom. It's not worth turning yourself into, you know....

DEE-DEE

Are you going to stick up for me now? Be all, like, solidarity? It's a little late, you've already fucked up everything!

SAM

I didn't mean to fuck things up, I just, I....

DEE-DEE

Oh, you were helping us out when you did whatever it is you did, when you hired a private eye or whatever to check up on me?

SAM

No ... I told you, it wasn't my fault.... I just happened to see it, because of my boyfriend....

DEE-DEE

Yeah, right, *what* boyfriend! There's no way that out of a billion porn sites you just happened on the one with *me* in it! When I only ever did it just a couple of times *ever!* Just tell the truth if that's what you're so fucking into!

SAM

All right, so I had you looked into! I hired someone to look into you! I just did it as a.... I didn't think he would find anything! I was just mad and worried and I wanted to make myself feel better! And then when he ... and then once he found out about the websites I was stuck! I *had* to tell, then! What do you want, you want me to say that I regret having done it? Well, I do. I wish I didn't know and was never going to find out and that I could just fly out here and be *normal.* The whole flight out here, I was on that plane, I felt like I'd put a noose around my neck and had jumped off a chair. The whole flight over here was like that nanosecond between when you step off the chair and when your neck snaps, that nanosecond where you say to yourself, "Wait, no, are you nuts?! What are you doing?!" Except that it hasn't been a nanosecond, it's been days and days and days, and.... Is that what you wanted me to say? Are you happy now?

DEE-DEE

No, I'm not happy, I'm not happy because you've fucked up everything!

TOM

No, *you've* fucked up everything, you've *fucked* everything, you are a fucking fucking fucking cunt whore, and I want you to *GET THE FUCK OUT OF MY HOUSE!*

(Tom grabs Dee-Dee by the arm and shoulder and roughly marches her out; Sam runs after a little ways, but stops before the door; she grabs at Tom, ineffectually.)

SAM

Tom! Don't hurt her!

(Exit Tom and Dee-Dee. For a moment Sam looks off to where Tom and Dee-Dee have exited. She sits. She stands. Fidgets. Sits, starts to read a text on her Blackberry. Can't. She stands, paces. Pauses. Enter Tom, suddenly, walking straight at her, fast.)

SAM

Tom!

TOM

You fucking bitch.

(Tom shoves Sam; she lands on her ass.)

SAM

Tom! What's gotten into you!

TOM

Fucking meddling bitch!

SAM

Are you crazy?! I.... *Tom!*

TOM

Get the fuck out of here!

SAM

What's gotten into you!

TOM

I don't want to see you again, ever! Ever!

(Sam scrambles to her feet and out of Tom's reach.)

SAM

Tom....

TOM

I'm serious. Get outta here or I'll kill you.

SAM

Tom.... I only wanted to be a good sister....

TOM

I don't want to see you again. I will kill you. I don't want to ever, ever see you again.

SAM

Oh, Tom....

(Exit Sam. Tom stares after her, clenching and unclenching his fists. Paces around. His rage begins to melt—he starts to cry.)

TOM

Dee-Dee, Dee-Dee. Oh, Dee-Dee.

(Tom stands, hands over his face, getting control of himself. He looks at the laptop. Sits down, opens it, refreshes the page. Turns up the volume. We can hear people on the website fucking.)

TOM

Dee-Dee. Dee-Dee. Dee-Dee.

(As the lights go down, the soundtrack of heavy breathing and raunchy porn sex rises. The volume gets louder and louder until the effect is ominous and almost abstract; phase shifts are added as we slip into total darkness.)

END

ABOUT THE AUTHOR:

J. Boyett is a playwright, novelist, filmmaker, and founder of Saltimbanque Books. Please visit www.saltimbanquebooks.com or jboyett.net, and sign up for the mailing list.

J. Boyett can also be reached at:
jboyettjboyett@gmail.com.

If you enjoyed this book, please help support it by rating it on Amazon, Goodreads, and any other online forum.

And we hope you'll go to saltimbanquebooks.com and sign up for our mailing list.

Thanks!

ALSO FROM SALTIMBANQUE BOOKS:

THE VICTIM (AND OTHER SHORT PLAYS), by J. Boyett

In The Victim, April wants Grace to help her prosecute the guys who raped them years before. The only problem is, Grace doesn't remember things that way.... Also included:

A young man picks up a strange woman in a bar, only to realize she's no stranger after all;

An uptight socialite learns some outrageous truths about her family;

A sister stumbles upon her brother's bizarre sexual rite;

A first date ends in grotesque revelations;

A love potion proves all too effective;

A lesbian wedding is complicated when it turns out one bride's brother used to date the other bride.

RAW FLESH, COLD AIR, by J. Boyett

Eighth-grader Sam Peabody's boyfriend (well, not exactly boyfriend) asked her to text him a picture of her boob, so she did. But then her not-really-boyfriend didn't keep it to himself.

So now her life is sorta ruined. But things will get better. After all, the civilized adults charged with Sam's care won't leave her to writhe in hell indefinitely, all on account of a dumb text. Right?

THE SWITCH, by J. Boyett

Beth used to be a powerful witch, till a meth addiction burned her powers away. Her daughter Farrah thinks she's nothing but a loser. But Beth thinks maybe Farrah would change her mind if she had to spend a few days in her mom's shoes—and when she gets her hands on a new source of magic, she decides to make that happen....

THE SEXBOT, by J. Boyett

The AI Revolution has come, and it ain't easy for a single dad to find a decent job. Most things that a human can do, a computer can do better and cheaper. So Brad provides for his kids as best he can, using virtual reality to remote-control a sexbot in a brothel. Male, female, straight, gay: Brad the anonymous operator does it all. A man's got to provide.

But even the brothel gig is barely enough to scrape by on. So when his kids' guidance counselor Duane shows up as a customer, Brad wonders if he can use this chance encounter to build a better future for his children?

STEWART AND JEAN, by J. Boyett

A blind date between Stewart and Jean explodes into a confrontation from the past when Jean realizes that theirs is not a random meeting at all, but that Stewart is the brother of the man who once tried to rape her.

COLD PLATE SPECIAL, by Rob Widdicombe

Jarvis Henders has finally hit the beige bottom of his beige life, his law-school dreams in shambles, and every bar singing to him to end his latest streak of sobriety. Instead of falling back off the wagon, he decides to go take his life back from the child molester who stole it. But his journey through the looking glass turns into an adventure where he's too busy trying to guess what will come at him next, to dwell on the ghosts of his past.

I'M YOUR MAN, by F. Sykes

It's New York in the 1990's, and every week for years Fred has cruised Port Authority for hustlers, living a double life, dreaming of the one perfect boy that he can really love. When he meets Adam, he wonders if he's found that perfect boy after all ... and even though Adam proves to be very imperfect, and very real, Fred's dream is strengthened to the point that he finds it difficult to awake.

THE MAN WHO FED MYAGG'DAGGETH, by J. Boyett

Will is compelled to have sex with a new woman every few days.

No, really. Will has a demon inside him, literally, and if he fails to periodically satisfy a woman, he'll explode. Literally.

Unfortunately, every successful tryst passes the infection along to his unwitting partner. Women in the New York area are starting to blow up.

How far will William go in his dehumanizing, destructive struggle to stay alive?

Answer: pretty damn far.

TUSK, by J. Boyett

One year ago, Britney and Riley survived the onslaught of the monster, Tusk. They lived, but at the moment of their escape Britney disgraced herself.

Now, Tusk is back, and Britney has a chance at redemption—whether she wants it or not....

RESILIENT CREATURES, by J. Boyett

Journey to worlds both horrific and humdrum in this collection from J. Boyett: Aliens are discovered and nobody cares; the origin of ferrets is revealed; alternate sexualities are explored; a new appreciation of the woes of vampirism is cultivated; an unfortunate lady has a superfluity of eyes; and so on, and so forth....

AMY MADDEN, by J. Boyett

Amy Madden haunts the town of Hutchins. But who or what is Amy Madden?

IRONHEART, by J. Boyett

Part H.P. Lovecraft and part Alien, Ironheart is the story of what happens when the mining ship Canary comes across a strange derelict on the edge of the galaxy—a derelict occupied by a strange and seemingly immortal woman....

RAY TAKESHI AND THE MEDALLIONS OF SKARTH, by J. Boyett

Ray Takeshi doesn't remember his parents--they died in sorcerous battle, when he was just a baby. He's been raised in Missouri by a mage named Ned. Ned says his Destiny approaches: a final test, to determine whether Ray will achieve manhood, or be destroyed.

Just because Ray is a fledgling mage doesn't mean he buys such mumbo-jumbo. But then the delectable succubus Melania von Fleiden shows up in town, alongside her hideous Thrall. Ray has to stop her evil plan--or die trying, at least. Could this be that test Destiny was sending? And if so, does he have the slightest chance of surviving it?

THE UNKILLABLES, by J. Boyett

Gash-Eye already thought life was hard, as the Neanderthal slave to a band of Cro-Magnons. Then zombies attacked, wiping out nearly everyone she knows and separating her from the Jaw, her half-breed son. Now she fights to keep the last remnants of her former captors alive. Meanwhile, the Jaw and his father try to survive as they maneuver the zombie-infested landscape alongside time-travelers from thirty thousand years in the future.... Destined to become a classic in the literature of Zombies vs. Cavemen.

THE LITTLE MERMAID: A HORROR STORY, by J. Boyett

Brenna has an idyllic life with her heroic, dashing, lifeguard boyfriend Mark. She knows it's only natural that other girls should have crushes on the guy. But there's something different about the young girl he's rescued, who seemed to appear in the sea out of nowhere—a young girl with strange powers, and who will stop at nothing to have Mark for herself.

BENJAMIN GOLDEN DEVILHORNS, by Doug Shields

A collection of stories set in a bizarre, almost believable universe: the lord of cockroaches breathes the same air as a genius teenage girl with a thing for criminals, a ruthless meat tycoon who hasn't figured out that secret gay affairs are best conducted out of town, and a telepathic bowling ball. Yes, the bowling ball breathes.

RICKY, by J. Boyett

Ricky's hoping to begin a new life upon his release from prison; but on his second day out, someone murders his sister. Determined to find her killer, but with no idea how to go about it, Ricky follows a dangerous path, led by clues that may only be in his mind.

BROTHEL, by J. Boyett

What to do for kicks if you live in a sleepy college town, and all you need to pass your courses is basic literacy? Well, you could keep up with all the popular TV shows. Or see how much alcohol you can drink without dying. Or spice things up with the occasional hump behind the bushes. And if that's not enough you could start a business....

DAUGHTER OF THE DAMNED, by J. Boyett

Before Carol was born, Harold ruined her mother's life. Now Carol's out for vengeance, with the help of the bounty hunter Snake.

But her quest has set off a trap left by her mother. And Carol and her mother's old enemy will have to team up, if either wants to get out alive.

www.ingramcontent.com/pod-product-compliance
Lightning Source LLC
LaVergne TN
LVHW010104110826
845155LV00028B/480

9781941914205